THE USBORNE

ART
TREASURY

With original artwork by Vincent van Gogh,
Katsushika Hokusai, Hendrick Avercamp,
Pablo Picasso, unknown African artists,
Paul Klee, Henri Rousseau, Alexander Calder,
Henri Matisse, James Whistler, Claude Monet,
Vassily Kandinsky, Shen Quan, Edgar Degas,
Alberto Giacometti, Damien Hirst,
Johnny Bulunbulun, Georgia O'Keeffe,
Jackson Pollock, unknown Iranian artists,
JMW Turner and Richard Long

Project artwork by Abigail Brown,
Nicola Butler, Mary Cartwright, Katie Lovell,
Sam Meredith, and Non and Daisy Taylor

Cartoons by Georgien Overwater

Edited by Abigail Wheatley and Jane Chisholm
Managing designer: Mary Cartwright
Picture research by Ruth King
Digital manipulation by John Russell

THE USBORNE
ART
TREASURY

Rosie Dickins

Designed by Nicola Butler

With thanks to Dr. Erika Langmuir, OBE
for expert information and advice

Contents

Introduction

This book has a fascinating collection of art from around the world. It has masks from Africa, prints from Japan, and paintings and sculptures from Europe. You can read about each work of art and the artist who made it, and then try out a project inspired by it. Some of the projects show you how to use the same method or materials. Other projects are based on what the artwork shows, so you can explore the same themes and ideas.

Water Lilies - Morning

painted by Claude Monet between 1914 and 1918

This picture is one of a series, designed to line a room, showing the pond from dawn to dusk.

About Monet

Claude Monet was born in France in 1840. As a young artist, he spent most of his time painting outdoors – whether it was sunny fields, windy beaches or snowy roads. Whatever the weather, he wanted to be on the spot to study the changing light.

At first, people laughed at Monet's style. They thought his pictures were far too rough and sketchy. But, by the time he died in 1926, he was one of the world's most successful artists, with whole galleries devoted to his work.

This calm scene shows the pond in Claude Monet's garden at Giverny in France. Monet designed the pond himself, and painted it again and again over thirty years. He filled huge canvases with rapid dabs of paint, trying to capture the effect of sunlight on water. His loose, sketchy style creates a dreamy atmosphere, full of ripples, reflections and glowing lilies.

Monet would go to great lengths to get the perfect view. He sat on rocking boats, climbed rickety ladders and even dug trenches to stand in.

48   49

Read about a famous water lily picture, built up out of layers of paint – then try making your own lilies using layers of coloured tissue.

What you will need

Most artists work in studios, where they have space to make and store things. But a table or floor covered in newspaper, and a box for your art materials, will do just as well. It's a good idea to read through each activity before you start, to check you have everything you will need. Here is a list of the materials used in the projects in this book:

- ❋ Coloured paper, plain paper and tissue paper
- ❋ Giftwrap and newspaper
- ❋ Cardboard, felt and scraps of fabric
- ❋ Pencils, felt-tip pens and ink
- ❋ Chalks or chalk pastels
- ❋ Wax crayons and oil pastels
- ❋ Watercolour paint and acrylic paint
- ❋ Ready-mix paint and poster paint
- ❋ Paint brushes in different sizes
- ❋ PVA glue, sticky tape and a glue stick
- ❋ Silver foil, glitter and string or raffia
- ❋ A plastic fork and a drinking straw
- ❋ A paper plate, a cardboard box and a pin
- ❋ Cotton wool, pipe cleaners and poster putty
- ❋ A sponge, a toothpick and some salt
- ❋ Polystyrene from packaging

the Starry Night

painted by Vincent van Gogh in 1889

Van Gogh once said, "looking at the stars always makes me dream."

8

This picture shows a dramatic night sky with twinkling stars and twisting trees. The scene has been built up out of layers of paint so thick, you can see the brush marks in it. The artist, Vincent van Gogh, liked to use strongly coloured paint, often straight from the tube. His intense colours and swirling brush strokes make his pictures vivid and full of movement.

About van Gogh

Vincent van Gogh was born in Holland in 1853. By the age of 27, he had tried teaching, shop work and preaching, all without success. Then, he decided to devote himself to art. But he struggled to make a living and managed to sell only one painting during his life. Today his pictures are worth millions.

Sadly, van Gogh suffered from mental illness. In one famous incident, he cut off part of his left ear after arguing with a friend. By 1889, he was in a mental hospital. He continued to paint furiously, but became more and more depressed. A year later, he shot himself.

Swirly landscape

Vincent van Gogh created his landscape with dramatic swirls and curls built up of thick layers of paint. You can try this swirly technique for yourself using thick acrylic paints.

1. On thick paper, sketch a landscape with rolling hills, leafy trees and a swirling, cloudy sky.

The glue makes the paint thicker.

2. Squeeze out some acrylic paints onto a plate. Mix a few drops of PVA glue into each blob.

3. Paint blue and white swirls for a cloudy sky. Don't worry if you go over the lines of your sketch.

You could scrape some short lines to look like grass.

4. Scrape a plastic fork around the curves of the clouds and sky, to make swirly marks in the paint.

5. Paint hills and trees in browns, greens and yellows. Wipe the fork, then scrape wavy lines along the hills.

6. Finally, use the tip of a paintbrush handle to scrape round curls into the tree tops.

The Great Wave off Kanagawa

created by Katsushika Hokusai between 1823 and 1829

This print was made by carving a picture onto wooden blocks – one block for each colour. The blocks were then coated with ink and pressed onto paper.

This Japanese print is full of drama, with tiny boats being tossed on stormy seas. A huge wave is about to crash over the boats, claws of foam reaching for the sailors. The wave is so big, it seems to dwarf the distant peak of Mount Fuji.

Floating World

In Japan, scenes like this are known as ukiyo-e, or "pictures of the floating world". They are meant to celebrate the fragile beauty of ordinary life. Often, they show popular actors, fashionable women or landscapes with people going about their daily lives, such as these sailors.

About Hokusai

Katsushika Hokusai was born in Tokyo in 1760. He was apprenticed to a printmaker, but experimented so much he was thrown out. Stubbornly, he kept on experimenting and became very successful. In fact, his most popular prints sold so many copies that the blocks used to make them wore out.

The print will be a
mirror image of your
original drawing.

Sea print

Hokusai printed his towering wave using sea-blue inks on white paper. These steps show you how you can create your own stormy sea print in blue and white.

Draw big, curly waves.

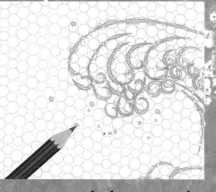

1. Draw a sea scene on a flat piece of polystyrenc from a pizza box or some protective packaging.

2. 'Carve' the scene by pushing a sharp pencil into the sheet. Do this many times along each line.

3. Dot some holes around the edges of the waves. Brush off any loose pieces of polystyrene.

4. Mix some blue poster paint and sponge it over the polystyrene. Lay a piece of paper on top.

5. Rub all over the paper with your hand, keeping your fingers flat. Then, lift off the paper.

A Winter Scene with Skaters near a Castle

painted by Hendrick Avercamp in about 1608-09

This 400-year-old Dutch painting shows a busy winter landscape. All kinds of people are out walking in the snow or skating across the ice – or falling over. There is even a snowball fight going on.

Imaginary castles

At the time of this picture, there was a craze for landscape paintings. The artist, Hendrick Avercamp, specialized in winter scenes. He lived in Holland and based his pictures on the countryside and people around him. The result looks incredibly lifelike, but it isn't all real. The castle with the pink tower existed only in Avercamp's imagination.

These close-ups show some of the skaters in more detail. Notice their bulky winter clothes.

About Avercamp

Hendrick Avercamp was born in the Netherlands in 1585 and spent most of his life in the sleepy little Dutch town of Kampen. He was known as the "mute of Kampen" because he was deaf and dumb. But his disability didn't stop him from studying art in Amsterdam and selling his pictures across Europe.

Winter trees

Bare trees tower over Avercamp's picture, making it feel cold and wintry. This project shows you how to create your own winter trees using runny paint and a drinking straw.

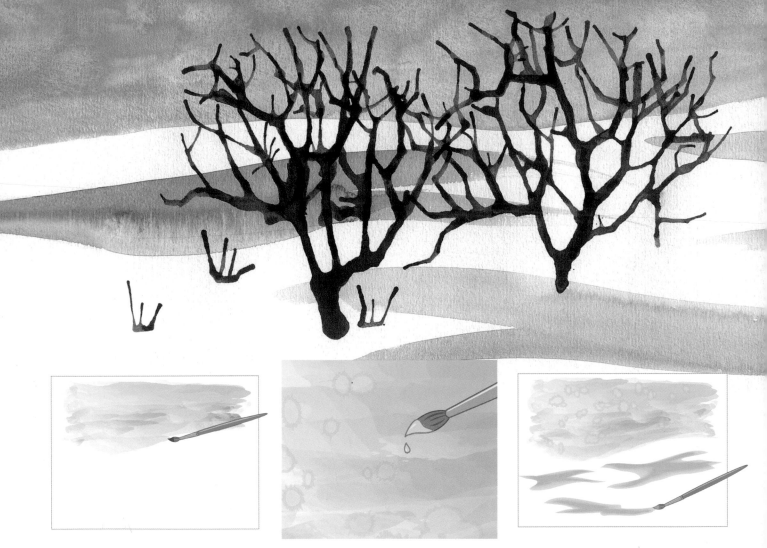

1. Dilute blue ready-mix paint to make it watery, and brush it onto a piece of white paper, for a sky.

2. Before the paint dries, dip a brush in water and let it drip over the sky, to spread the paint.

3. Dilute brown ready-mix paint to make it watery. Paint the ground, leaving white patches showing.

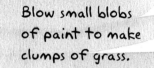

Blow small blobs
of paint to make
clumps of grass.

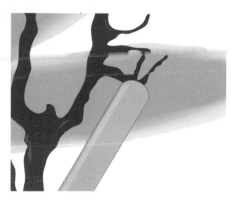

4. When the paint is dry,
dilute brown ready-mix
paint to make it runny.
Dab a blob on the ground.

5. Blow on the blob
through a drinking
straw, so the paint flows
up and makes a trunk.

6. Use the end of the
straw to pull lines of
paint out of the trunk.
Blow them into branches.

Clown collage

Picasso made dozens of clown pictures and invented the technique of collage (sticking things onto his pictures). This project shows you how to make your own blocky clown collage, using different papers and fabrics.

1. On a piece of thick paper, paint a stage and a curtain. Leave it to dry.

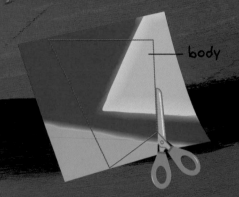

body

2. From paper or fabric, cut a half-circle head, and a blocky body like this.

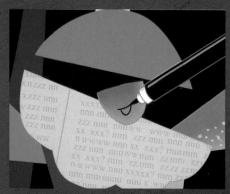

arms

legs

3. Cut out two triangles for arms, two for legs and four tiny ones for hands and feet.

ruff

4. Cut out a curvy ruff, like this, and a half-circle and a triangle for a hat.

5. Arrange the pieces on top of the painted stage and glue them down.

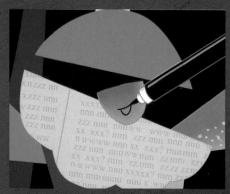

6. Stick on more cut-out shapes for decoration. Add details with a felt-tip pen.

Mix materials – such as painted
newspaper, giftwrap or felt –
for different patterns and textures.

Cardboard mask

African masks are carved in wood and carefully decorated. This project shows you how to make your own mask by cutting and decorating thick, corrugated cardboard from a box.

You can buy raffia from specialist art and craft shops, florists or garden centres.

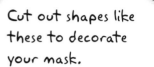

Cut out shapes like these to decorate your mask.

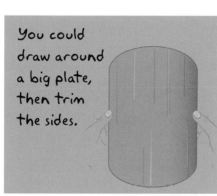

You could draw around a big plate, then trim the sides.

1. Draw a simple face shape on some corrugated cardboard and cut it out. Bend it into a curve.

2. Draw two dots about halfway down. Carefully push a sharp pencil through the card to make eyeholes.

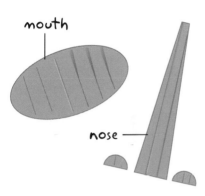

mouth

nose

3. From more cardboard, cut a long triangle and two half-circles for a nose, and an oval for a mouth.

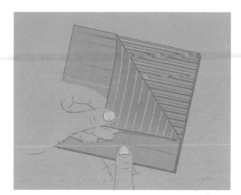

4. Peel the top layer off some more cardboard. Cut out two half-ovals for eyes, from the bumpy part.

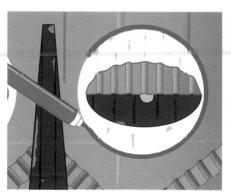

5. Cut out more shapes. Glue all the shapes onto the mask and decorate it with paint or felt-tip pens.

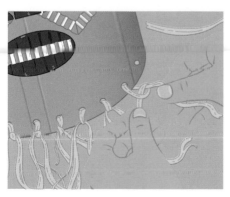

6. Make holes around the chin. Poke short pieces of raffia or string through the holes and knot them on.

Magical creatures

Paul Klee created magical fish pictures using watercolour and oil paints. You can create a similar effect with watercolour paints and oil pastels or wax crayons.

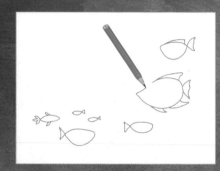

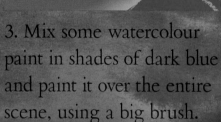

The pastels or crayons will show through the paint.

1. Lightly sketch some sea creatures on thick white paper. Add some plants and squiggles around them.

2. Fill in the creatures with bright oil pastels or wax crayons. Draw over the plants and squiggles, too.

3. Mix some watercolour paint in shades of dark blue and paint it over the entire scene, using a big brush.

You could add a jungle animal based on a sketch of your pet.

Jungle scene

Rousseau used glowing colours and strong shadows to bring his jungle painting to life. Now you can create your own jungle, with dramatic shading and brightly coloured fruit.

1. On a piece of thick pale blue paper, draw a jungle scene with overlapping branches, leaves and fruit.

2. Mix some watercolour paint in dark green and fill in some of the branches and leaves.

3. Let the paint dry. Then, fill in the rest of the leaves and branches, and the ground, with black ink.

Fill in the top half of the leaf.

4. When the ink is dry, mix some orange watercolour paint and fill in the fruit. Wait until that dries, too.

5. Draw a line along the middle of every black leaf, using a dark green pencil. Shade in half of each leaf.

6. Shade half of each green leaf with a light green pencil. Outline the oranges in red pencil and add dots.

Eleven Polychrome

This artwork gets its name from the eleven multi-coloured or "polychrome" shapes.

created by Alexander Calder
in 1956

Nowadays, mobiles are mass-produced and sold in shops around the world. But, in the 1930s, they were a brand new idea. The inspiration came from an artist named Alexander Calder. He wanted to create sculptures which moved – but without machinery. The result was the first mobile.

36

Catching the breeze

This mobile is designed to hang in mid-air and
catch the breeze. It is made of moving branches
tipped with metal shapes. The branches are
heavy, but their weight is balanced so
it takes only the slightest breath of
wind to make them drift and turn.

Calder once said, "To most people
who look at a mobile, it's no more
than a series of flat objects that move.
To a few, though, it may be poetry."

About Calder

Alexander Calder was born in America in 1898.
He came from a family of artists and he
set up his own workshop at the age
of eight, making tiny moving
animals out of metal. Although
he studied to be an engineer,
he soon returned to art. He is
best known for his mobiles,
but he also made fixed sculptures,
which he called "stabiles".

One of Calder's first grown-up works of
art was a toy circus with moving performers.

37

Hanging mobile

Alexander Calder created huge mobiles out of painted steel and wire. This project shows you how to make a miniature version using cardboard and pipe cleaners.

1. Take six different-sized pipe cleaners and bend the ends down to make curved "arms" like this.

2. Take one arm and bend one end around to make a loop. Thread a second arm through the loop, like this.

Use the shorter pipe cleaners lower down.

3. Add five of the arms in the same way. When you thread on the bottom arm, don't loop its ends.

Make seven matching pairs of shapes like this.

4. Fold some thick paper in half. Draw a curvy shape, then cut around it, through both layers of paper.

The matching shape goes on top of the pipe cleaner.

5. Tape one shape under the free end of an arm. Glue the matching shape on top. Do this six more times.

6. Loop string around the top arm and hang up the mobile. Bend the arms around until they balance.

Hang your mobile
somewhere it can
move in the breeze.

the Sorrows of the King

created by Henri Matisse in 1952

In real life, this picture is nearly twice as high as a man and fills an entire wall.

Hari Matisse
1952

This cut-paper collage shows a king sitting on a raised platform, playing a guitar. Another musician crouches at his feet and a woman dances before them. The colourful patterns create a cheerful effect – like the music and dancing, which are meant to distract the king from his sorrows.

Drawing with scissors

Henri Matisse became famous for his paintings. But when he made this picture, he was too ill to stand up at an easel and paint. Instead, he began to create scenes with shapes cut out of paper. He called this "drawing with scissors", but it is usually known as collage.

This photograph shows Matisse in bed, cutting out shapes for a picture.

About Matisse

Henri Matisse was born in 1869 in France. He was going to be a lawyer, but then fell ill. While he was recovering, his mother bought him a box of paints to keep him entertained – and he was hooked. As soon as he was well again, he gave up law and trained to become an artist.

Colourful collage

Henri Matisse loved making colourful pictures about music and movement. You can create your own version with this cheerful collage.

1. Cut out some large rectangles from colourful paper, such as old magazines or giftwrap.

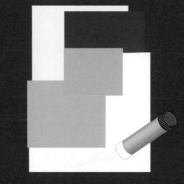

2. Glue the rectangles onto a sheet of paper, so they overlap and cover it completely.

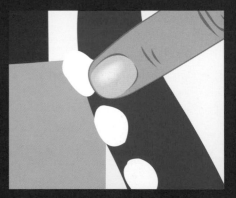

saxophone

end piece

3. Draw a wavy saxophone shape and an oval end piece, like this. Carefully cut around the shapes.

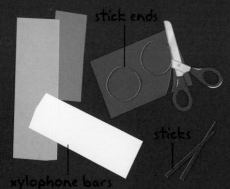

stick ends

sticks

xylophone bars

4. Cut out small rectangles to make a xylophone. For xylophone sticks, cut two thin strips and two circles.

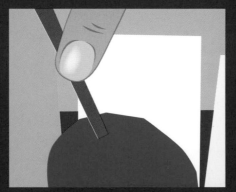

5. Arrange the instruments on top of your picture and glue them down. Glue the xylophone sticks on last.

6. Draw some tiny oval shapes. Cut them out and glue them onto the saxophone to make its keys.

Try adding stars and
wavy strips around
the instruments,
to suggest sounds.

Spattery fireworks

Whistler conjured up the feel of a firework display out of a smudge of smoke and a scatter of bright sparks. You can recreate this effect using sponged and spattered paint.

1. Draw a low horizon line on a piece of purple paper. Lay your paper on plenty of newspaper.

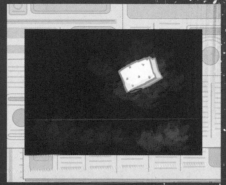

2. Use a sponge to dab some pink and orange poster paint in patches above and below the line.

3. Rinse the sponge. Press its flat side into dark purple paint, then print a blocky shape above the line.

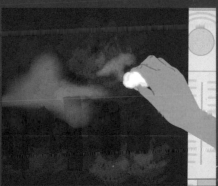

4. Print more blocky shapes above and below the horizon line, for buildings and their reflections.

5. When the paint is dry, use cotton wool to smudge on purple and yellow chalk pastel or chalk, for smoke.

6. Mix some runny paint in yellows and reds. Dip in a brush, hold it over the paper and flick the bristles.

Colour contrasts

Kandinsky created a striking picture using circles in contrasting colours. Try it for yourself using watercolour paints and oil pastels or wax crayons.

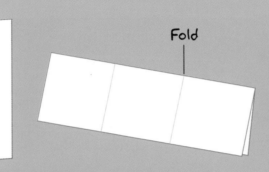

Fold

1. Fold a piece of paper into three equal sections, like this. Pinch the creases, then unfold the paper.

2. Then, fold the paper in half lengthways. Pinch the crease and unfold it. The creases make six squares.

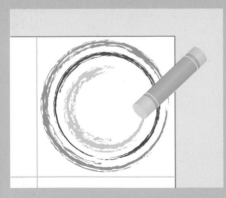

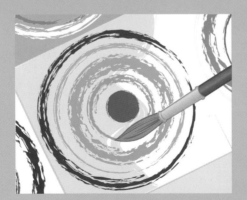

3. Using oil pastels or wax crayons, draw some rings inside each square. Leave gaps between the rings.

4. Paint over the squares with watercolour paint, using a different colour for each square.

The oil pastels or wax crayons show through the paint and create colourful contrasts.

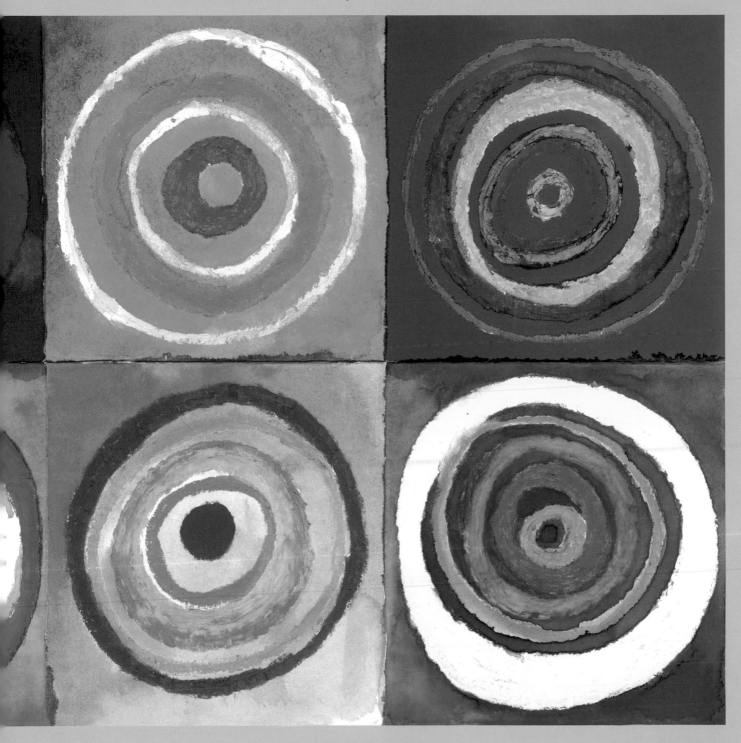

Pastel dancers

Degas used soft pastels to capture the delicate fabric of his dancers' costumes. You can use chalk pastels or chalks to create a similar effect.

1. On rough brown or black paper, sketch an oval head and a curved neck in chalk pastel or chalk.

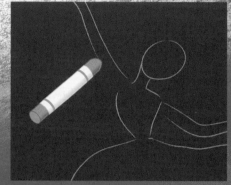

2. Draw on a triangular body and a wide, round ballet dancer's skirt. Add some gently curving arms.

3. Colour in the skin and add pink cheeks. Smooth over the skin tones with your finger.

Colour the background too.

4. Fill in the dress with shades of blue, green and lilac. Work out from the waist, using short strokes.

5. Finally, add some sleeves, hair, eyes and lips, and any small details like roses and flowing ribbons.

You could add legs with
pointed ballet shoes,
if you have space.

Foil figures

Alberto Giacometti sculpted hundreds of stick people in different poses. You can sculpt your own stick people using pipe cleaners and silver foil.

— twist here

twist here —

1. Twist the ends of two pipe cleaners together to make a pair of legs. Keep twisting to form a body.

2. Crumple up a small ball of paper. Loop the middle of another pipe cleaner over the ball and twist it tight.

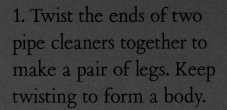

3. Place this piece at the top of the body for a head and arms. Wind each arm twice around the body.

4. Roll two balls of poster putty and push the legs into them. Squash them so the figure stands up.

Try bending the
arms and legs into
different positions.

For a dog, use shorter
pipe cleaners and add
two small pieces to
make the ears and tail.

5. Cut some strips of silver
foil. Wrap them around
all the pipe cleaners,
then scrunch them tight.

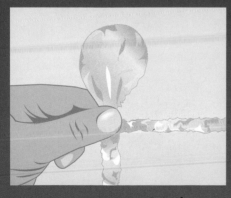

6. Cut a square of foil.
Crumple it over the head,
pinching it tight around
the neck.

Spin-painted plate

Damien Hirst creates his spin pictures on a huge wheel.
You can try a similar technique by spinning a paper plate.
It's very messy – so watch out for flying paint.

The box will help to catch any flying drips of paint.

1. Find a shallow cardboard box, bigger than a paper plate. Stick a ball of poster putty in the middle of it.

Push the pin in from the front of the plate.

2. Stick a square of sticky tape to the middle of the back of a paper plate. Push a pin through both layers.

3. Put the plate in the box and push the pin into the putty. Try spinning the plate – it may stick at first.

4. Dilute some different colours of poster paint, to make them runny. Dribble some paint over the plate.

For smaller patches of colour flick paint from a brush.

5. As the paint falls, spin the plate. Keep dribbling and spinning, using different colours of paint.

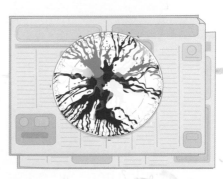

6. Lift the plate out of the box and leave it flat on some old newspaper until it is completely dry.

This painting was created on dried tree bark by Aboriginal artist Johnny Bulunbulun. Aboriginal peoples were the first to live in Australia, with a history going back thousands of years. Bulunbulun painted the picture in the traditional Aboriginal way, using natural earth colours and brushes made from twigs or grass.

Family art

Bulunbulun's painting reflects Aboriginal beliefs. It shows Australian animals gathering to drink from a waterhole. To Aboriginal peoples, the waterhole is sacred because it represents the source of life. A row of bats hangs from the top of the picture, long-necked turtles and geese gather below, and snakes twist between them. These animals all feature in Aboriginal myths and ceremonies.

About Bulunbulun

Johnny Bulunbulun was born in the 1940s, in a remote part of northern Australia known as Arnhem Land. The land and animals from where he grew up are very important in his work. As well as painting, he is famous for his singing and takes part in traditional Aboriginal ceremonies.

For the finishing touch, think of a title for your painting. Does it remind you of anything?

Bark painting

created by Johnny Bulunbulun between 1960 and 1995

Leave a brown strip showing around the edge.

Scratched animals

J ohnny Bulunbulun painted his animals on textured bark. You can get a similar effect by painting onto a torn piece of rough brown paper or cardboard.

Light colours work best.

1. Tear out a rectangular piece of cardboard or paper. Cover it with stripes of colour, using oil pastels.

2. Mix some dark acrylic paint with a little water. Then, paint over the pastel so it is completely covered.

Alternatively, you could draw an animal shape first, and just fill that in with pastels and paint.

The oil pastel shows through the scratches.

3. When the paint is almost dry, use a toothpick to scratch different animal shapes and patterns into it.

Petal collage

Georgia O'Keeffe specialized in smooth, delicate flower pictures. This project shows you how to make a poppy picture using different colours of smooth paper.

1. Fold some red paper in half, and in half again. On the top layer of paper, draw a wide petal shape.

2. Cut around it, through all the layers of paper. Use darker paper to make small petals in the same way.

3. Fold some green paper in half. Draw a leaf, like this. Cut around it, through both layers of paper.

4. Arrange the petals and leaves on a large sheet of coloured paper. Then, glue them in place.

5. Cut out a small oval and a cross in contrasting colours, and glue them in the middle of your flower.

You could add a ring of tiny
drop shapes around the middle
using paper or a felt-tip pen.

Sparkly tiles

The glittering Iranian tiles were decorated with specialized, glass-based glazes. But you can also get a sparkly "glazed" effect by using PVA glue and glitter.

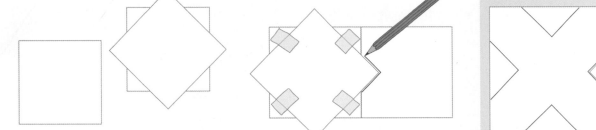

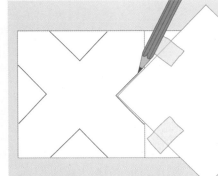

1. Cut three identical squares of cardboard. Overlap two of them to make a star shape.

2. Tape the star together. Place the star along one edge of the third square and draw around the point.

3. Do the same along each edge of the square, so you have the outline of a cross. Cut it out.

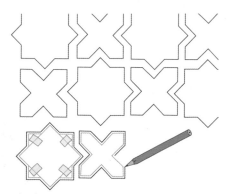

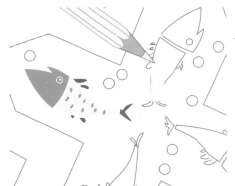

4. Place the cross and star onto a sheet of paper and draw around them. Do this until the paper is covered.

5. Draw animals and plants inside the paper shapes. Colour them in with pencils or crayons.

6. Mix some PVA glue with water and stir in a spoonful of glitter. Brush the glue all over the tiles.

When the glue is dry, cut out your tiles
and arrange them so that they tessellate.

Stormy seas

Turner painted many atmospheric views of skies and seas. This project shows you how to paint your own stormy sea picture using watercolours – which Turner often used himself.

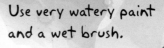
Use very watery paint and a wet brush.

1. Lightly sketch a ship in a storm on thick white paper. Fill in the ship, using a dark wax crayon.

2. Wipe a wet sponge over your paper. Then, mix some watercolour paint in pale blues and greens.

3. Brush streaks of blue and green diagonally all over the sea and sky. Let the streaks run together.

The salt makes watery marks.

4. Mix some watercolour paint in darker blues and greens. Streak it under the ship and across the sky.

5. Sprinkle patches of salt on top of the wet paint. Leave the picture to dry, then shake off the salt.

6. Use a white chalk pastel or chalk to add flecks of foam on the waves and lines of rain in the sky.

Handprint circles

Richard Long made his handprint circles straight onto a wall. You probably won't be allowed to paint on a wall, so this project explains how to create handprint circles on paper.

Use a pencil.

1. Draw around a big plate on a big piece of paper. Squeeze some ready-mix paint onto an old plate.

2. Press your hand flat into the paint. Then, press your hand onto the paper at the edge of the circle.

Wash your hand before each new colour.

3. Squeeze different colours of paint onto more plates. Make more hand prints all around the circle.

4. Now, make another ring of hand prints inside the first. Leave a slight gap between the rings.

When the paint is dry, erase the pencil ring.

Every effort has been made to trace the copyright holders of the material in this book. If any rights have been omitted, the publishers offer their sincere apologies and will rectify this in any subsequent editions following notification. The publishers are grateful to the following organisations and individuals for their contributions and permission to reproduce material:

Cover: *The Starry Night* by van Gogh, see credit for pages 8-9. **Pages 6-7:** *Waterlilies – Morning* by Monet, see credit for pages 48-49. **Pages 8-9:** *The Starry Night* (1889) by van Gogh, oil on canvas, 74 x 92cm © (2006) The Museum of Modern Art (MoMA), New York/ Lillie P. Bliss Bequest/ Scala, Florence. **Pages 12-13:** *The Great Wave off Kanagawa* by Hokusai, colour woodcut, 25 x 38cm © Historical Picture Archive/ CORBIS. **Pages 16-17:** *A Winter Scene with Skaters near a Castle* (c.1608-09) by Avercamp, oil on wood, 41 x 41cm © The National Gallery, London. **Pages 20-21:** *Punchinello with a Guitar* (1920) by Picasso, oil on canvas © Private Collection/ The Bridgeman Art Library/ Succession Picasso/ DACS 2006. Photograph of Picasso and his son Claude in 1955 © Bettmann/ CORBIS. **Pages 24-25:** *Songye Mask* (19th century) by an unknown artist, painted wood © The Art Archive/ Private Collection/ Dagli Orti (A). *Kuba Mask* (19th century) by an unknown artist, painted wood and straw © The Art Archive/ Private Collection/ Dagli Orti (A). **Pages 28-29:** *The Golden Fish* (1925) by Klee, oil and watercolour on paper and board, 50 x 69cm © Hamburger Kunsthalle, Hamburg, Germany/ The Bridgeman Art Library/ DACS 2006. **Pages 32-33:** *Monkeys in an Orange Grove* (1910) by Rousseau, oil on canvas, 111 x 163cm © Private Collection/ The Bridgeman Art Library. Photograph of Rousseau in his studio © Edimédia/ CORBIS. **Pages 36-37:** *Eleven Polychrome* (1956) by Calder, sheet metal, wire and paint © Christie's Images/ CORBIS/ Estate of Alexander Calder/ ARS, NY and DACS, London 2006. **Pages 40-41:** *The Sorrows of the King* (1952) by Matisse, gouache on canvas, 292 x 386cm © Musée National d'Art Moderne, Centre Pompidou, Paris, France/ The Bridgeman Art Library/ Succession H. Matisse/ DACS 2006. Photograph of Matisse © akg-images/ Bianconero. **Pages 44-45:** *Nocturne in Black and Gold, the Falling Rocket* (c.1875) by Whistler, oil on wood, 60 x 47cm © The Detroit Institute of Arts, USA/ Gift of Dexter M. Ferry Jr./ The Bridgeman Art Library. **Pages 48-49:** *Waterlilies – Morning* centre right section (1914-18) by Monet, oil on canvas, 200 x 425cm © Musée de l'Orangerie, Paris, France/ Lauros/ Giraudon/ The Bridgeman Art Library. **Pages 52-53:** *Squares with Concentric Circles* (1913) by Kandinsky, watercolour, gouache and black chalk, 24 x 32cm © ARTOTHEK/ ADAGP, Paris and DACS, London 2006. **Pages 56-57:** *Cat* (1747) by Shen Quan, ink on paper © Christie's Images/ CORBIS. Brush strokes by Evelyn Ong. **Pages 60-61:** *Dancers in Blue* (c.1897) by Degas, pastel on paper © Archivo Iconografico, S.A./ CORBIS. **Pages 64-65:** *The Square* (1948-49) by Giacometti, bronze, 59 x 45 x 25cm © Private Collection/ Lefevre Fine Art Ltd., London/ The Bridgeman Art Library/ ADAGP, Paris and DACS, London 2006. **Pages 68-69:** *beautiful, sharp, screaming, subtle, ice-cream-ish, yikes, gosh with pinks painting (with rosy orange centre)* (1995) by Hirst, gloss household paint on canvas, 214cm diameter © Damien Hirst, courtesy Jay Jopling/ White Cube (London). **Pages 72-73:** *Bark painting* by Bulunbulun © Penny Tweedie/ CORBIS/ VISCOPY, Australia/ DACS 2006. **Pages 76-77:** *Jimson Weed* (1932) by O'Keeffe, oil on canvas, 122 x 102cm © (2006) The Georgia O'Keefe Museum, Santa Fe/ Dono della Fondazione Burnett/ Fondazione Georgia O'Keefe/ Art Resource/ Scala, Florence/ ARS, NY and DACS, London 2006. **Pages 80-81:** *Lavender Mist* (1950) by Pollock, oil, enamel and aluminium paint on canvas, 221 x 300cm © National Gallery of Art, Washington DC, USA/ The Bridgeman Art Library/ ARS, NY and DACS, London 2006. Photograph of Pollock © Time & Life Pictures/ Getty Images. **Pages 84-85:** *Wall panel of star- and cross-shaped tiles depicting birds, animals and figures, Islamic, from Kashan in Central Iran* (c.1250-1300) by unknown artists, 79 x 50cm © Louvre, Paris, France/ Peter Willi/ The Bridgeman Art Library. **Pages 88-89:** *The Fighting Temeraire* (1839) by Turner, oil on canvas, 91 x 122cm © The National Gallery, London. **Pages 92-93:** *Mud Hand Circles* (1989) by Long, 320cm diameter, courtesy of the artist and Haunch of Venison, photograph by kind permission of the Master and Fellows, Jesus College, Cambridge.